# Tales of Blood, Folly, and Love

Kit Karlsson

BookLeaf
Publishing

Presentation by *BookLeaf Publishing*

Web: www.bookleafpub.com

E-mail: info@bookleafpub.com

ISBN: 9789357615730

First edition 2022

# Mr. Nobody

Still, it's nice to be wanted
to know that somewhere
there's a cold hand to touch me
a ghost in the air.

And every grey morning
is not half so drear
with his whispered 'Hello—
how are you, my dear?'

Ah, it's nice to be haunted
by one so polite
in the jaws of the city
this monstrous night.

# The Cry of the Selkie

She always said it must be so.

The moon-white sea
the sun-gold snow
the paw of brock
and blood of crow
these are the things
the Grey Folk know.

And I, and I
will always be
a little star
in a lonely sea
and still the Selkie
calls to me.

She said, quite cool, she killed a man.

It didn't matter
how or when
and if she saw
his face again
his skull, his flaming soul in hell
she'd make his blood run
thick and fell.

And I, and I
and oh, I see
the folly of
all things to be
and still the Selkie
cries to me.

She said she loved me—never mind.

The Greyling son
she left behind
shudders at
the Selkie kind.
He draws his bath
and drinks his tea
the water calls
unceasingly.

And why, oh why
this dreadful skin?
The seven tears
are sinking in.
I cannot linger
dare not stay
the Selkie calls
us all away.

# Queen of the Underworld

It's really not such a bad gig after all.
Her mother sends cocoa and apples each fall
her husband adores her, and the little black dog
licks her hand with three tongues. A pearly grey
fog
of souls flits around her; their bodies below
make compost for stars and flowers to grow.
Death is no fear, Death is no pain
Death is quite simply a long day of rain
after which many green things will blossom
again.

# The Bear Man

The little lame man
with the black boots
came calling again for Jack today.
'Ho, Jack!' he said, in his merry way.
'It's been ten long years, you're free now--
free to cut your hair, cut your nails
take a bath, marry your girl!
And all the gold I promised
will be yours now at last.'

Well, Jack scooped him up
and peeled him like an apple
put him in a pot of beans
he had in the fire-pit for supper.
(The boots he left for the magpies
who had a great fondness for silver buckles.)

What had he to do
with the world of men anymore?
His girl was fat, and shrill, and had three
children
with another man.
Gold he had no use for
unless it was golden honey

in which case, he always asked the bees quite
politely
if they would care to share a comb or two with
him.


He ate his beans that night, in a warm little cave
in the green wood
and admired his long hair.
And then he took a long bath in the lake
for soap was the one thing, more than his soul
that he had really missed.

# The Call

And really, it's my biggest fear
that when you call, I won't be here
you left so many notes for me
in summer sky and galaxy
in ziggurat and jungle tomb
in standing stone and desert rune—
and oh, I saw, just yesterday
you're wanted by the CIA
I don't suppose they'll find you, though
you make it hard enough, you know
I get so scared and lonely when
I think you might not come again
I love you, mom. I miss you too.
Maybe I should come find you.

# The Reluctant Princess

I mean, what if I don't want to kiss him?
He's cute enough as a frog, isn't he?
And anyway, catching flies is a good deal less
unpleasant
than the sort of thing
a man usually expects you to do.

# The Green Wood

'Oh, my love, if ever I could
I'd follow you to the wild green wood
I fear no beast nor the roar of the pine
for the touch of your lips is sweeter than wine.'

'There's a fever upon him,' the doctor said.
'He's talking at night to the unholy dead.'
'There's a curse on this town,' said old Father
John
'and there's no telling where all the children
have gone.'

'Oh, my love, won't you come follow me?
I will make you sweet cakes of honey and cream
I will bring you fine roses to crown your fair
head
I'll bedevil your soul and sweeten your bed.'

'There's a sickness upon us,' the doctor cried
and that night dashed himself from the
mountainside.
'There's nothing to do,' the old Blackrobe said
and that night in shame and fear he fled.

'Oh, my love, to the green wood I fly

and no man can stop me--no man dare try
I fear no beast nor the roar of the pine
for the touch of your fang is sweeter than wine.'

# Beans

Chopped down that old yellow vine
in the vegetable patch today
and I must say, it was rather peculiar—
an arrogant little fellow, the size of my thumb
was crawling upon it.
He declared he had come to steal my goose
and seduce my wife
and so, quite naturally, I squished him.
Perhaps if he had asked nicely
I wouldn't have minded giving him
a nice juicy leaf or a drop of honeydew for his
trouble.
But they're all the same, the miserable pests
and so I have to keep spraying the beans.

# The Passage

The angel comes at midnight
I'll be waiting in my bed
I've made a little salad
and I've baked a little bread.
Father marked the door with blood—
I wiped it all away.
The angel comes at midnight
and I've no great wish to stay.

# Metamorphosis

She takes tea with the ladies, very polite
and none of them knows that every night
she peels off her face and hangs up her skin.

'Darling,' she says, 'how have you been?'
She makes him a cocktail when he comes home
she plays bridge with his friends, and chats on
the phone.

The men praise her charms, her sly, green-eyed
air
their wives admire her hands and her hair
the boys make up stories, the girls like to
pretend.

She is everyone's muse, and nobody's friend.
She laughs, and she says she is doing OK
but it hurts just to breathe every day.

# Medicine Hat

'Medicine Hat
Medicine Hat
have you a cure for me?'

'Belladonna, my son
take three leaves with your tea.'

'Medicine Hat
Medicine Hat
shall I be rich some day?'

'Arsenic, my son
keeps the devils away.'

'Medicine Hat
Medicine Hat
where did I lay my bride?'

'Down in the cellar
where the mandrakes hide.'

'Medicine Hat
Medicine Hat
what can you give me for this pain?'

'Wolfsbane, my son
and you shall never weep again.'

# Camp

But it really doesn't feel like death at all.
It feels like I'm the girl in that old horror show
driving down a country road
on a sunny day
with a handsome stranger
in a sleek black car
trailing inexorably behind—
and Mr. Serling scolding me
because I don't seem to be sufficiently afraid.

# The Changeling

It's all right—I know you well
I know the sort of lies you tell
I like your face, your hair, your eyes
it's really quite a nice disguise
but underneath those clever lies
I know you're scared and lonely, too
and all you really want to do
is feel like someone cares for you.
Don't you fret—I'll never tell
come and rest here for a spell
we Fairy Folk keep our secrets well.

# The Wife of the Prophet

Will you be my bride in the summertime, will
you come to the desert with me?
Will you leave your father and brother behind,
and all of your finery?
I cannot buy you pretty frocks, nor shoes for
your little white feet
I live in a cave by the brush on the rock—no
lights, no water, no heat.

But I will make you your own fine bed, a bed of
soft sweet hay
I will gather primrose and clover for your hair,
and crown you every day
and many good things grow in the desert, good
and wholesome to eat
I will bring you orange blossoms and honey, and
melons and peccary meat.

Oh, it's not such a hard thing to be poor, after
all, when the river sings you to sleep
when the moon is your mother and father, and
the stars are red and deep
when your own little world is filled with gold,
the gold of the sun and the sand

when your own pretty wife is lying beside you,
and holding your hard brown hand.

# The Wife of the Prophet: Part II

Today was the day of fury and flame—the
papers predicted the end
the Sheriff called in the Army Reserve and his
Vietnam special-ops friend
they dragged the man from the cave where he
slept and filled his heart with lead
they shot the dogs and both of the kids and
bombed the old lookout shed.

They found her down by the riverside, after the
fire died down
she was wearing a crown of flowers and a
simple blue homespun gown
the Sheriff wept for his daughter—he cursed the
Prophet's name
they buried the bodies deep in the cave and
burned the film when the newsmen came.

# Loki

I conjure thee by the Nine Spirits
by bone of fish and wing of bird, I conjure thee
by the sacred herb, I conjure thee.

Oh Lord of Mischief
deign once again to return to me
after a long night of revelry
with some she-devil in the woods
after a long day of hunting
the foul Muridae
after day and night of weary travel
I bid thee come, my King.

For my hearth is ever thy home
even though thou hast been
a very naughty cat.

# Birthday Wishes for the Master

By all the fair things under heaven
by all the foul things down in hell
my your candles burn ever brighter
may you never be sad or unwell.

May you find a fair maiden whose blood
runs thicker and richer than rain
may the wind not disturb your ashes
may you never feel hunger or pain.

May the sunlight fade at your doorstep
may the chickpeas be withered and few
may the garlic die in a blight
and I hope your cake is nice, too.

# Quantum Ghosts

Bones will turn to dust and crumble
flesh will wither and decay
but the energy inside you
never fades away.

www.ingramcontent.com/pod-product-compliance
Lightning Source LLC
LaVergne TN
LVHW050308200726